PHOTOGRAPHIC MEMORIES

Francis Frith's
AROUND BARNSTAPLE

◆

Dennis Needham

FRITH
BOOK Co

First published in the United Kingdom in 1999 by
Frith Book Company Ltd

British Library Cataloguing in Publication Data

Around Barnstaple
Dennis Needham
ISBN 1-85937-084-5

Frith Book Company Ltd
Frith's Barn, Teffont,
Salisbury, Wiltshire SP3 5QP
Tel: +44 (0) 1722 716 376
Email: frithbook.co.uk

Printed and bound in Great Britain

CONTENTS

◆

FRANCIS FRITH: *Victorian Pioneer*

FRANCIS FRITH, Victorian founder of the world-famous photographic archive, was a complex and multitudinous man. A devout Quaker and a highly successful Victorian businessman, he was both philosophic by nature and pioneering in outlook.

By 1855 Francis Frith had already established a wholesale grocery business in Liverpool, and sold it for the astonishing sum of £200,000, which is the equivalent today of over £15,000,000. Now a multi-millionaire, he was able to indulge his passion for travel. As a child he had pored over travel books written by early explorers, and his fancy and imagination had been stirred by family holidays to the sublime mountain regions of Wales and Scotland. 'What a land of spirit-stirring and enriching scenes and places!' he had written. He was to return to these scenes of grandeur in later years to 'recapture the thousands of vivid and tender memories', but with a different purpose. Now in his thirties, and captivated by the new science of photography, Frith set out on a series of pioneering journeys to the Nile regions that occupied him from 1856 until 1860.

INTRIGUE AND ADVENTURE

He took with him on his travels a specially-designed wicker carriage that acted as both dark-room and sleeping chamber. These far-flung journeys were packed with intrigue and adventure. In his life story, written when he was sixty-three, Frith tells of being held captive by bandits, and of fighting 'an awful midnight battle to the very point of surrender with a deadly pack of hungry, wild dogs'. Sporting flowing Arab costume, Frith arrived at Akaba by camel seventy years before Lawrence, where he encountered 'desert princes and rival sheikhs, blazing with jewel-hilted swords'.

During these extraordinary adventures he was assiduously exploring the desert regions bordering the Nile and patiently recording the antiquities and peoples with his camera. He was the first photographer to venture beyond the sixth cataract. Africa was still the mysterious 'Dark Continent', and Stanley and Livingstone's historic meeting was a decade into the future. The conditions for picture taking confound belief. He laboured for hours in his wicker dark-room in the sweltering heat of the desert, while the volatile chemicals fizzed dangerously in their trays. Often he was forced to work in remote tombs and caves where conditions were cooler. Back in London he exhibited his photographs and was 'rapturously cheered' by members of the Royal Society. His reputation as a photographer was made overnight. An eminent modern historian has likened their impact on the population of the time to that on our own generation of the first photographs taken on the surface of the moon.

VENTURE OF A LIFE-TIME

Characteristically, Frith quickly spotted the opportunity to create a new business as a specialist publisher of photographs. He lived in an era of immense and sometimes violent change. For the poor in the early part of Victoria's reign work was a drudge and the hours long, and people had precious little free time to enjoy themselves.

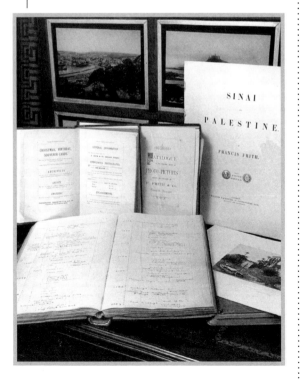

Most had no transport other than a cart or gig at their disposal, and had not travelled far beyond the boundaries of their own town or village. However, by the 1870s, the railways had threaded their way across the country, and Bank Holidays and half-day Saturdays had been made obligatory by Act of Parliament. All of a sudden the ordinary working man and his family were able to enjoy days out and see a little more of the world.

With characteristic business acumen, Francis Frith foresaw that these new tourists would enjoy having souvenirs to commemorate their days out. In 1860 he married Mary Ann Rosling and set out with the intention of photographing every city, town and village in Britain. For the next thirty years he travelled the country by train and by pony and trap, producing fine photographs of seaside resorts and beauty spots that were keenly bought by millions of Victorians. These prints were painstakingly pasted into family albums and pored over during the dark nights of winter, rekindling precious memories of summer excursions.

THE RISE OF FRITH & CO

Frith's studio was soon supplying retail shops all over the country. To meet the demand he gathered about him a small team of photographers, and published the work of independent artist-photographers of the calibre of Roger Fenton and Francis Bedford. In order to gain some understanding of the scale of Frith's business one only has to look at the catalogue issued by Frith & Co in 1886: it runs to some 670

pages, listing not only many thousands of views of the British Isles but also many photographs of most European countries, and China, Japan, the USA and Canada – note the sample page shown above from the hand-written *Frith & Co* ledgers detailing pictures taken. By 1890 Frith had created the greatest specialist photographic publishing company in the world, with over 2,000 outlets – more than the combined number that Boots and WH Smith have today! The picture on the right shows the *Frith & Co* display board at Ingleton in the Yorkshire Dales. Beautifully constructed with mahogany frame and gilt inserts, it could display up to a dozen local scenes.

POSTCARD BONANZA

◆◆◆

The ever-popular holiday postcard we know today took many years to develop. In 1870 the Post Office issued the first plain cards, with a pre-printed stamp on one face. In 1894 they allowed other publishers' cards to be sent through the mail with an attached adhesive halfpenny stamp. Demand grew rapidly, and in 1895 a new size of postcard was permitted called the

court card, but there was little room for illustration. In 1899, a year after Frith's death, a new card measuring 5.5 x 3.5 inches became the standard format, but it was not until 1902 that the divided back came into being, with address and message on one face and a full-size illustration on the other. *Frith & Co* were in the vanguard of postcard development, and Frith's sons Eustace and Cyril continued their father's monumental task, expanding the number of views offered to the public and recording more and more places in Britain, as the coasts and countryside were opened up to mass travel.

Francis Frith died in 1898 at his villa in Cannes, his great project still growing. The archive he created continued in business for another seventy years. By 1970 it contained over a third of a million pictures of 7,000 cities, towns and villages. The massive photographic record Frith has left to us stands as a living monument to a special and very remarkable man.

Frith's Archive: *A Unique Legacy*

FRANCIS FRITH'S legacy to us today is of immense significance and value, for the magnificent archive of evocative photographs he created provides a unique record of change in 7,000 cities, towns and villages throughout Britain over a century and more. Frith and his fellow studio photographers revisited locations many times down the years to update their views, compiling for us an enthralling and colourful pageant of British life and character.

We tend to think of Frith's sepia views of Britain as nostalgic, for most of us use them to conjure up memories of places in our own lives with which we have family associations. It often makes us forget that to Francis Frith they were records of daily life as it was actually being lived in the cities, towns and villages of his day. The Victorian age was one of great and often bewildering change for ordinary people, and though the pictures evoke an impression of slower times, life was as busy and hectic as it is today.

We are fortunate that Frith was a photographer of the people, dedicated to recording the minutiae of everyday life. For it is this sheer wealth of visual data, the painstaking chronicle of changes in dress, transport, street layouts, buildings, housing, engineering and landscape that captivates us so much today. His remarkable images offer us a powerful link with the past and with the lives of our ancestors.

TODAY'S TECHNOLOGY

Computers have now made it possible for Frith's many thousands of images to be accessed almost instantly. In the Frith archive today, each photograph is carefully 'digitised' then stored on a CD Rom. Frith archivists can locate a single photograph amongst thousands within seconds. Views can be catalogued and sorted under a variety of categories of place and content to the immediate benefit of researchers. Inexpensive reference prints can be created for them at the touch of a mouse button, and a wide range of books and other printed materials assembled and published for a wider, more general readership - in the next twelve months over a hundred Frith local history titles will be published! The

See Frith at www. francisfrith.co.uk

day-to-day workings of the archive are very different from how they were in Francis Frith's time: imagine the herculean task of sorting through eleven tons of glass negatives as Frith had to do to locate a particular sequence of pictures! Yet the archive still prides itself on maintaining the same high standards of excellence laid down by Francis Frith, including the painstaking cataloguing and indexing of every view.

It is curious to reflect on how the internet now allows researchers in America and elsewhere greater instant access to the archive than Frith himself ever enjoyed. Many thousands of individual views can be called up on screen within seconds on one of the Frith internet sites, enabling people living continents away to revisit the streets of their ancestral home town, or view places in Britain where they have enjoyed holidays. Many overseas researchers welcome the chance to view special theme selections, such as transport, sports, costume and ancient monuments.

We are certain that Francis Frith would have heartily approved of these modern developments, for he himself was always working at the very limits of Victorian photographic technology.

THE VALUE OF THE ARCHIVE TODAY

Because of the benefits brought by the computer, Frith's images are increasingly studied by social historians, by researchers into genealogy and ancestory, by architects, town planners, and by teachers and schoolchildren involved in local history projects. In addition, the archive offers every one of us a unique opportunity to examine the places where we and our families have lived and worked down the years. Immensely successful in Frith's own era, the archive is now, a century and more on, entering a new phase of popularity.

THE PAST IN TUNE WITH THE FUTURE

Historians consider the Francis Frith Collection to be of prime national importance. It is the only archive of its kind remaining in private ownership and has been valued at a million pounds. However, this figure is now rapidly increasing as digital technology enables more and more people around the world to enjoy its benefits.

Francis Frith's archive is now housed in an historic timber barn in the beautiful village of Teffont in Wiltshire. Its founder would not recognize the archive office as it is today. In place of the many thousands of dusty boxes containing glass plate negatives and an all-pervading odour of photographic chemicals, there are now ranks of computer screens. He would be amazed to watch his images travelling round the world at unimaginable speeds through network and internet lines.

The archive's future is both bright and exciting. Francis Frith, with his unshakeable belief in making photographs available to the greatest number of people, would undoubtedly approve of what is being done today with his lifetime's work. His photographs, depicting our shared past, are now bringing pleasure and enlightenment to millions around the world a century and more after his death.

BARNSTAPLE – *An Introduction*

DEVON IS USUALLY associated with crowds of noisy holidaymakers wearing silly hats and eating ice cream. You will not find anything like this in Barnstaple, for this sturdy town lies in the north of England's second largest county.

Developed alongside the river Taw, Barnstaple is located to the west of Exmoor and north of Dartmoor. These two natural barriers meant that until the railways pointed their iron fingers towards the town relatively late in the Railway Age, access was difficult and few made the effort. Thus this feeling of being cut off from the rest of the country - until Victorian times at least - created an altogether different culture.

This feeling was not altered for most the 20th century. Where the rest of the country was moving rapidly to the culture of the car, motorways and heavy traffic were alien to north Devon. It was not until the 1980s that a major road was provided, replacing a twisting narrow old highway that was built to handle horse-drawn traffic originally. The great car-borne invasion of the 1960s and 1970s simply did not happen in North Devon. Motorways were just a new word in the dictionary, and even today there is less than two miles of dual carriageway throughout the region.

All this has created a somewhat insular culture in the area - one that pervades to some degree to this day. It is not difficult to find someone who has never been abroad, or never even visited London. Slow and gentle in both speech and mien, the true Devonian is a delightful person, not yet wholly corrupted by modern life.

For all that, Barnstaple has an absorbing history. Fifty miles to the south, on the northern slopes of Dartmoor, the river Taw rises. A few miles short of the sea, the river Yeo joins and it was here that a settlement was established; but as to the date of the town's founding, historians have debated for years without a satisfactory answer. Athelstan was supposed to have granted a charter in to the town in 930, making it the oldest borough in England. Millenary celebrations were held here in 1930, which had the effect of setting the date in stone. Many scholars, however, feel that Alfred the Great was instrumental in creating a fort here to defend against Danish insurgents. One point beyond dispute is that Athelstan established coin minting here.

Whoever is correct, there was a substantial settlement at the time of Domesday. New charters were granted in 1154 and 1189, and the town continued to grow both in size and importance. Its location close to the estuary, but well sheltered from it, was assuming increasing importance; for several hundred years, Barnstaple's history was one intimately connected with the sea and seafaring.

In 1588, the town sent five ships to join Drake in overcoming the Spanish Armada. Commerce was flourishing at this time, but would not do so for much longer. The estuary was already prone to silting, and getting ships to Barnstaple Quay was becoming increasingly difficult. A new Quay had been built around 1550, although there was a degree of flood prevention work involved rather than providing extra berthing accommodation for ships. Despite the increasingly difficult passage, freight was still delivered to the town by water well into the 20th century.

Ships have been built alongside the river for generations, even if the earliest records only go back to 1743. One of the larger yards - Westacott's - started trading in the early years of the 19th century and built many substantial vessels which sailed around the world. Traditional work ceased in the 1880s but there was a brief reprise during the Great War.

Ferro-concrete was being considered as a boat-building material, and several barges were built in the town. The engineer in charge was Percy Westacott, grandson of the shipbuilder. Sadly, after a series of mishaps, the project was scrapped. Nothing daunted, the company - now in private hands - started to build small steel coasters. Post-war demand shrivelled and the factory closed.

One other factor that increased the importance of Barnstaple was that it had a bridge over the river. Known as The Longbridge, it was already in existence by 1200; the exact date when it was built is unknown. It seems that unusually for the time, all the sixteen arches were built of stone. It is also possible that the platform nearest to Barnstaple was built to form a drawbridge. Longbridge was originally constructed as a packhorse bridge with large refuges to allow walkers to escape the horses. Over the centuries, it has been progressively widened and strengthened, but its historical significance was confirmed in 1937 when it was classified as an Ancient Monument.

One event that has made Barnstaple famous throughout Devon is its Fair. This has been held since time immemorial. It started off as a celebratory event after the huge annual market which lasted for a week. Horses, other livestock and produce were traded, and even farm labourers found new positions here. Today, the livestock market is held every Friday, and the Pannier Market - so called because the original stallholders would bring their produce to market by horse in panniers - every Tuesday and Friday. The fair still takes place, but is essentially an event within the modern meaning of the word. A large collection of showmen and their rides assemble during September, and the town becomes hyper-active for a few days.

The railway from Exeter arrived in 1854 and from Taunton in 1873. The main station was on the west of the river, the one that survives to this day. It became known as Barnstaple Junction a few years later when the line to Ilfracombe was opened. This involved building a spindly iron bridge over the Taw alongside the Longbridge. Immediately on reaching the far side, a station - Barnstaple Quay - was opened. This lasted until 1898 when the narrow gauge railway to Lynton was built. There was no room to bring this line into Quay station, so the station closed, re-located a few yards further along the Quay and was re-named Barnstaple Town. Famous trains including The Devon Belle crossed the river here, and a direct service to London Waterloo left several times each day. The Town station buildings are still intact, although the line to Ilfracombe closed in 1970.

Other services from Barnstaple Junction station linked the town with Bideford, Torrington and Halwill Junction (for Bude and other Cornish stations). They were pro-gressively closed, with the last service to Bideford running in 1965. Today, the railway, a pale shadow of its former self, has a single carriage trundling to Exeter and back, up to seven times each day.

One large price that was paid for accom-modating the Lynton line was that North Walk disappeared. This was an attractive area of parkland and lake, built where the Yeo runs into the Taw. For many years, Barnstaple Fair was held here. The mound of earth that was once Barnstaple Castle was also included in this area: a lovely amenity area lost to the town over a century ago. This feeling of loss endures today, for the Civic Offices stand out like the proverbial sore thumb. The architects surely qualify for an award for creating 'a Site of Outstanding Natural Ugliness'.

There was one other station - Victoria - which handled the Great Western services from Taunton across Exmoor. This was a ter-minus - in Victoria Road - and services for Ilfracombe departed in the opposite direc-tion before crossing the Taw to reach Junction station. This was closed in 1966, although the goods depot building still remains, converted to other uses.

The omnibus was first seen in the town in 1919 when Colwill's started a service to Braunton and Ilfracombe. By 1922, services were so numerous that a new bus station was needed. This was built in The Strand, along-side what was the site of Quay station. As a matter of historic record, this station served the needs of Barnstaple's bus travellers until July 1999 when a new station was opened on Queens Street.

Celebrity status has never fitted comfort-ably on the shoulders of Barnstaple citizens. Few locals have made their names known to a wider audience. One particular exception is John Gay. He was born in the High Street in 1685, and educated at Barnstaple Grammar School before briefly moving to London. Having returned home, he began to write poetry and published a series of poems by subscription, earning himself the huge sum of £1,000 in 1720. But it was an idea suggested to him by Jonathan Swift, the satirist and author of 'Gullivers Travels', that made Gay's name famous. In 1728, he wrote 'The Beggars' Opera', which was set to music by the German composer Johann Christoph Pepusch using popular and traditional music.

The town is well blessed with fine build-ings, many erected during the Victorian era. Most have survived to the present day, and make exploration of Barnstaple a pleasing adventure. What is now the Queens Theatre has a fascinating history. It was built as The Music Hall in 1855. 'Musical' activity was con-fined to the first floor, while the ground floor was used as a corn market. It was re-named The Albert Hall, then turned into a food store at the outbreak of the last war. Then in 1941 it caught fire, leaving only the shell. This was refurbished and became a British Restaurant, which was where war workers were fed. After hostilities ceased, it became the Civic Hall. It was finally rebuilt in 1952, taking the name of The Queens Hall. The original exterior walls were virtually the same as the day it was first built. In the early 1990s, an extensive re-fit inside turned it into The Queens Theatre. Local shows and touring companies offering both music and drama make up the annual playbill at this comfortable venue. As with many provincial theatres, there is a substantial subsidy needed; its future is the centre of debate as these pages went to press.

Pre-dating this period is the beautifully colonnaded Queen Anne's Walk, just off The Strand. Built in 1709, it housed the Exchange where merchants conducted their business. There is also a statue of the Queen. Restored several times over the years, the walk - especially in summer when hanging baskets of flowers adorn it - is a centre of attraction to this day.

Many other examples of fascinaing architecture are featured within these pages. One great pleasure still available to visitors is the ability to look around the town as it is today with the volume in your hands and still be able to recognise many of the scenes. Try standing where the photographer - probably with a huge box on a tripod and a black sheet for him to dive under - stood all those years ago, and reflect upon the old saw:

'The more things change, the more they remain the same'. This might well have been written to describe Barnstaple.

HAYMAKING 1890 24878
This photograph epitomises Devon a century ago.
Hay is being gathered at Chestwood by horse power;
traffic on the A39, which now roars across the valley
below, is a mere nightmare for the future. The
railway from Exeter is beyond the river to the left, the
Great Western line from Taunton is partially
concealed behind trees. The Long Bridge is in the
distance; the tall chimney is the brick works.

THE RIVER 1919 69315

All is tranquil a couple of miles up-river of Barnstaple. The L&SW railway follows the river almost from the watershed at Copplestone near Crediton, 30 miles away. The houses on the left are at Bishops Tawton; the riverside walk is still available for those who seek peace and solitude

THE BRIDGE 1890 24858

A superb study of the Long Bridge, taken at low tide. The iron supports of the railway bridge, just 25 years old at this time, are visible beyond. The building at the right hand end of the bridge is the Athenaeum, built in 1872. Next door (left) are Bridge End Buildings. These were demolished in 1962 when the bridge was last widened.

THE BRIDGE 1929 82267
Taken from the south shore, this view features two attractive clinker-built rowing boats still afloat as the tide streams out. Boating was extremely popular in this reach upstream of the bridge, a popularity which lasted until relatively recent times. Bale's Garage (now long gone) is clearly visible in The Square

THE IMPERIAL HOTEL 1903 49618
This view shows the river at low water, again with evidence of boating. The Imperial Hotel (centre left) has just completed a major expansion programme. Huge gilt letters that will be fixed to the guttering of the new portion are not yet in place. More views of this elegant hotel can be seen in photographs Nos 45717 & 64572 on pages 64 to 66. There is much activity just above the waterline: fishing was once a popular pastime on the river.

RIVERSIDE SCENE 1908 61066

Five years after the previous view was taken, the Imperial Hotel now boasts of its presence to the world. A high tide sees the recreational boats afloat. Strangely, no Edwardian Barumites (the local name for Barnstaple residents) are enjoying a summer walk along Taw Valley Parade. Note the weather recording station in the white box on the left.

RIVERSIDE SCENE 1912 64566

Leisure boating is completely absent in this photograph. A small collection of boys (extreme right) dressed exactly as one would expect of the era are doing what little boys have always done alongside rivers: enjoying themselves and getting filthy!

TRINITY CHURCH AND THE RIVER 1935
Holy Trinity church overlooks this tranquil river scene. Billy Moore's Boat Station - across the water - was built on a raft which floated up and down with the tide. You could hire rowing boats there, and at one time it was where Barnstaple Rowing Club had its base.

◆

FROM SOUTH WALK c1871
An early view of the bridge from the town side. Billy Moore's Boat Station (known to the local children as 'Noah's Ark') has still to make its appearance. Beyond the bridge, the sailing ship mast on the left is at Westacott's shipbuilding yard; those on the right are tied up at Barnstaple Quay. A small transom-sterned barge is beached by the slipway.

TRINITY CHURCH AND THE RIVER 1935 86658

FROM SOUTH WALK c1871 5826

THE PROMENADE 1890 24860
The Victorians loved their walks. This is The South Walk, on the town side of the river, with mother and children posing for the camera. Note the fashionable outfits they are wearing. This was also the area of Westacott's shipyard before they moved to below the bridge around 1846.

THE BRIDGE AND THE TERRACE 1890 24867
A nanny with her charge admires the view over the river. Note the three-wheeled push chair - back in fashion again a century later. This is Taw Vale Parade, a new road cut through what were the riverside gardens of the houses to the right.

SOUTH WALK 1894 33416
Here we see South Walk, with Old Moore's Boat Station now built. The area to the right is Rock Park. Beyond, the elegant town houses that once had rear gardens down to the river can be picked out through the trees.

FROM SOUTH WALK 1894 33415

With the river at about half tide, a collection of boys lounge in the river bed. A few hours ago, this was covered in sea water: the state of their clothing can only be guessed at. Whilst most of the boats appear to be pleasure craft, 'Rose' - nearest to the camera - was probably a fishing boat.

THE RIVER TAW AND SOUTH WALK 1899 43085

The Taw at high tide. The masts of sailing ships are visible beyond the bridge, and a fine collection of rowing boats can be seen around the boathouse. Left of the bridge is Shapland and Petter's Raleigh Cabinet Works, built in 1888 on the site of Westacott's old shipyard. Still in business today, the main output is wooden doors. The name 'Raleigh' refers to their previous premises in the town, which were burnt down.

THE RIVER TAW AND THE BRIDGE 1935 86659

By the time this picture was taken, the trees had gown to an enormous size and needed surgery. The river still provided scope for pleasure boating and Shapland & Petter's factory had grown to its full size. Today, boating is but a memory.

STICKLEPATH, SHOWING OLD BIDEFORD ROADS 1913 64570a

On the west bank of the Taw, this view shows the old road (left), and new one (right). The houses to the right are Ladysmith Villas, named after the second Boer War siege (1900). They still stand. Despite additional building and road widening, this scene is still easily recognisable, although a walk down the centre of the road (as the two men are doing) is not advisable.

DISTANT VIEW 1929

Taken close to Junction station, this photograph shows the North Devon Infirmary, the white building below the church tower. This opened in 1826, and lasted until a new one was built on the edge of town in 1978. The finger to the right of the tower on the river bank is an obelisk marking the opening of Rock Park.

VIEW FROM MOUNT SANDFORD 1929

An overview of Barnstaple taken from the Mount Sandford area. The lush fields are clear to see, as is the bridge, Raleigh Cabinet Works, and the estuary. The sandbars visible even at half tide illustrate why shipping to the town was lost.

DISTANT VIEW 1929 82257

VIEW FROM MOUNT SANDFORD 1929 82252

FROM ANCHOR WOODS 1919 69311
Anchor Wood is a narrow band of trees with a pleasant walk overlooking marshy ground downstream of the Long Bridge and at the foot of Sticklepath. The railway is the Bideford extension from Junction station. It lasted long after the passenger service was withdrawn, carrying coal to Yelland Power Station and ball clay from Peters Marland. Today it is a walking and cycle route, part of the 180 mile Tarka Trail.

ANCHOR WOODS 1919 69312
The Dripping Well in Anchor Woods was a popular spot with the Victorians. To the left, a kissing gate gives onto a path which now leads to the Tarka Trail. When the picture was taken, it led across the railway and round to the estuary before reaching Shapland and Petter's Raleigh Cabinet Works.

FROM ABOVE THE RAILWAY STATION c1871 5825
Our earliest view of Junction station. A small goods shed is to the left. The shaded area beyond the road will become the Ilfracombe railway. Several sailing vessels stand at Barnstaple Quay. Gas street lighting is already in place on the station approach road, but not on the Bideford road which leaves to the left.

FROM THE RAILWAY STATION 1894 33413

A detailed look at the station. To the right, a London & South Western Railway meat van waits to collect meat from the slaughterhouse (centre left). Shapland & Petters works is now built, served by rail from the Ilfracombe line behind the new houses (left). The 'chemical manure' factory has acquired a chimney. The furniture van (extreme left) is intriguing. The name 'Gillows' is the famous Lancaster furniture maker. Clearly, in pre-road transport days, it had not come from there. A local agent, collecting from the goods yard? Or even collecting sub-contract work from Shapland and Petter?

GENERAL VIEW 1919 69310

Taken from above Junction station, the jumble of old buildings in the foreground developed with the arrival of the railway. With the slaughterhouse, the 'chemical manure' factory and a railway engine shed, the houses to the left must have suffered greatly from smoke and smells emanating from this site.

DISTANT VIEW 1929 82256
A decade later, the scene has changed quite dramatically. The whole area has been razed and the railway sidings are clearly visible. The Osborne Hotel is across the road opposite the stations approach. The field in the foreground still produces hay: at least the farming was a constant. Today, the railway area is gone, given over to retail warehouses.

THE SQUARE 1903 49616
Long Bridge arrives from the right. Taw Vale Parade
is to the right of the Albert Clock, whose building
was started in 1862 and not completed until a
decade later; the money came from public
subscription. The other exit - left of centre - is
Lichdon Street. Note that electric street lighting is
already in place, only a few months after the
Barnstaple Corporation Electricity Works was
opened. The gazebo is a shelter for cabbies.

THE SQUARE 1912 64564

The horse is still the only means of propulsion, but changes are afoot. The old house to the left of the previous picture has been replaced by a car garage. Prideaux's were coach builders before the days of the horseless carriage. They were already agents for Humber and Rover cars. The gas light in the previous picture has had its lamp removed, replaced by a signpost. The base is unchanged. A small boy plays on the posts.

THE SQUARE 1935 86654

A dramatic change now, largely due to the spread of the internal combustion engine. Cars replace horses on the taxi rank, traffic lights control movement over the bridge, Prideaux's have expanded hugely, adding Morris and Austin to their dealerships, and the gazebo has gone, demolished by a runaway car. Trees behind the Albert Clock have been cut down to improve visibility, revealing the Imperial Hotel in the process. A man appears to be painting the posts on which the boy was playing in the last picture. He is old enough to have been that boy!

THE SQUARE 1929

Six years earlier, the traffic signals are not in place, nor are the bollards painted white. Note Bridge Buildings, vantage point for the three previous pictures. Most of the buildings are unchanged three quarters of a century later, although their use has altered. Lloyds Bank - to the right - is now a pub. The signpost is replaced by a tree.

◆

THE SQUARE 1929

An intriguing insight into the work of the photographer can be seen in the next two pictures. It is 4.30pm, and ladies' hats are de rigeuer in the Square. The building between the two Prideaux works is not yet in their hands as it would be six years later. After completing this picture, the photographer moved left . . .

THE SQUARE 1929 82259

THE SQUARE 1929 82262

THE SQUARE 1929 82260

. . . and, fifteen minutes later took this photograph. The bust - on a plinth to the left - is of Charles Sweet Willshire (1837-89), who was a liberal politician and municipal representative. Although still in this area, it has been re-located to the centre of the huge landscaped traffic island that dominates this scene today.

THE GARDENS AND THE SQUARE 1935 86653

Looking north into The Square, the taxi rank is still in the same place and little has changed save the fashions. An indication of the popularity of this area as a resort can be seen from the shop (extreme right) which is Mugford's Holiday Wear. Cycling is a popular pastime: note the number actually in use or standing by the roadside to the left to the Clock.

THE CLOCK TOWER c1955

The Athenaeum (left of centre) was built in 1872 as a private house for William Thorne. He died shortly after it was finished and William Rock bought it in 1888 to give to the town. It was the library for years, and today is home to the North Devon Museum.

THE FOUNTAIN AND CLOCK TOWER c1955

One clear change from previous views is the loss of the ornate iron railings around the whole area. They disappeared during the last War to be melted down for munitions. The Prideaux garage remains, although their agencies now seem to be Jaguar and Austin. Today, the site is occupied by The Bike Shed; the garage has moved to the edge of town as a Renault agent.

THE CLOCK TOWER c1955 B25065

THE FOUNTAIN AND CLOCK TOWER c1955 B25071

THE SQUARE c1955 B25067
From the roof of Bridge Building, a final look at this area, once the heart of Barnstaple. Holy Trinity church tower is prominent; to its left is a conical shaped roof. This was the pottery works of Charles Brannam, makers of Royal Barum Ware. Now demolished, the company operate a modern - and busy - factory on the edge of town.

THE STRAND, THE HORSE FAIR 1923 75164
Nothing could more illustrate the pace of change than this
photograph of the Horse Fair in 1923. Not only is the event a
distant memory, but there have been wholesale changes to the
area. The Angel Hotel (offering Good Stabling and Garage) was
knocked down and replaced by a cinema. This in turn has
become a nightclub. A pub built next door - The Bell - is now
derelict. The chimney in the background is at the electricity
works. This area is also the 'bus station; there are two charabancs
at the far end.

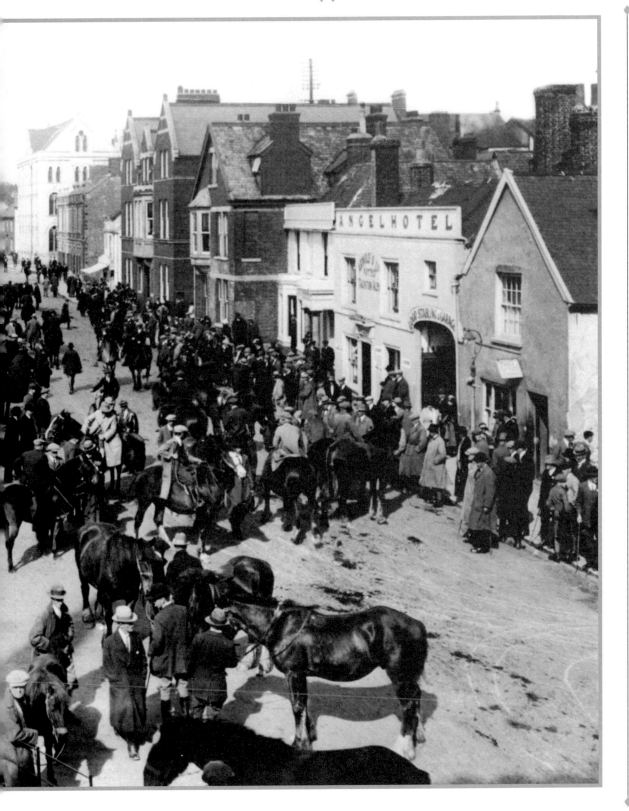

THE STRAND 1935 86655

A different kind of horsepower can now be seen in The Strand. Left of centre, with the elegant portico, is the 1922 bus station building. The Ilfracombe railway from Junction station arrives on the left. Here was the site of Quay station, moved a few hundred yards along by the time this picture was taken. The Bell Hotel, referred to in the caption to photograph No 75164 on pages 42 to 43, can be seen on the extreme right.

THE BUS STATION c1955 B25023

The bus station is still doubling up as a car park in this view, where a lone Southern National service awaits departure time. Railway signals can be seen behind and beyond the single-storied bus station building. Over the rooftop of the bus is the statue of Queen Anne.

QUEEN ANNE'S STATUE AND THE STATION 1890 24869

This gorgeously ornate building is early 18th-century, and has been refurbished every century since. Before the railway - the Quay station can be seen on the left - this area was quayside. Merchants have transacted their business here long before that. The statue of Queen Anne was given by Robert Rolle of Stevenstone in 1708. On the right, the Congregational Chapel was Victorian, although the church had been present in the town since 1662.

QUEEN ANNE'S WALK 1894 33419

The gas light in centre picture is wonderfully ornate. The assortment of gentlemen's wear ranges from smart business to working class layabout. On the right hand side there used to be a public washhouse and baths. At the time of this picture it was owned by the Masons. The Tone Stone, on which business deals were struck, is partially obscured in front of the centre arch. The inscription to the right is on the drill hall of the 4th Volunteer Battalion of the Devonshire Regiment.

QUAY STATION 1894 33414

Quay Station was the original town-side stop for the Ilfracombe train. When the narrow gauge line to Lynton was opened, there was insufficient room to bring it here and the station was moved a short distance along the quay. Venus soap is being advertised on the platform hoarding, and more enamel signs are attached to the riverside fence.

NORTH WALK LAKE 1894 33421

The Lake was filled in after the arrival of the railway. The island was known locally as 'Monkey Island', although its official title was Cypress Island. It seems rather sad that such a wonderful amenity should have met such as untimely end.

NORTH WALK 1890 24862
North Walk was destroyed when the Lynton and Barnstaple railway came through in 1898. Subsequently, a road was built linking The Strand with the end of High Street. The raised bank followed the Taw from Castle Quay and turned right to follow the Yeo to Braunton Bridge. This area was another example of the work of R D Gould, the borough surveyor.

ROLLE QUAY 1936 87549
Rolle Quay was the industrial area of Barnstaple,
located on the seaward side of the river Yeo. Even
in 1936, some trade is still in evidence. These ships
are tied up outside Richard Stanbury's Victoria
Flour Mill. The ship nearest camera was based at
Bridgwater in Somerset. On the right bank are the
remnants of the trees from North Walk.

PILTON PARK 1903 49626

This area exists today, still used for recreation. It was created from a raised area of ground where the river Yeo describes a large arc. Pilton was the original area of settlement before Barnstaple existed, and was cut off by bog and river until the 15th century. Note the wonderfully coloured bonnet worn by the child to the left.

HIGH STREET CORNER 1935 86657

The local policeman appears somewhat under-employed as he directs a single car travelling down Boutport Street towards The Square. Both Youings and The Royal and Fortescue are still in business, although the former has been rebuilt a couple of times. The billboard (extreme right) is advertising a Water Pageant with Decorated Floats. The High Street is on the left.

THE ATHENAEUM 1906 56044

This picture faces the opposite direction to the previous one. The cabman's shelter seen in photographs 49616 & 64564 on pages 34 to 36 is still in place. On the left, The Golden Lion was a 17th century merchant's house. Today it is called The Bank inn. This district was known locally as The Hearts of Oak

HIGH STREET 1894 33422

Taken almost from the bottom of High Street, many of these buildings are unchanged a century later, even if their uses have. Brook's Cafe Restaurant is now The Bradford & Bingley Building Society. The horse is still supreme: it would be another three years before the first car made its appearance in town. The cart on the right carries milk churns: deliveries of milk from a local farmer.

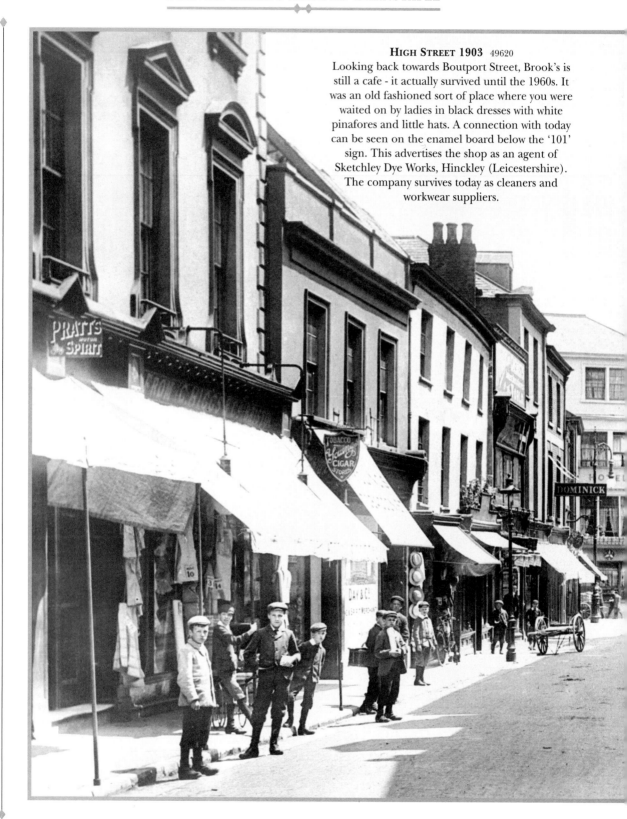

HIGH STREET 1903 49620
Looking back towards Boutport Street, Brook's is still a cafe - it actually survived until the 1960s. It was an old fashioned sort of place where you were waited on by ladies in black dresses with white pinafores and little hats. A connection with today can be seen on the enamel board below the '101' sign. This advertises the shop as an agent of Sketchley Dye Works, Hinckley (Leicestershire). The company survives today as cleaners and workwear suppliers.

HIGH STREET c1955 B25066

Further along the High Street, the local newspaper offices on the left have been rebuilt with some taste, which is more than can be said for the brick infill on the right that is Timothy Whites & Taylors. This is now a greetings card and toys shop. Yellow 'no waiting' lines do not yet disfigure the road surface.

HIGH STREET 1919 69320

Looking back down High Street towards Boutport Street at the bottom. Butchers Row is on the left. The Sydney Harper building is now a travel agent. Note that next door is another tradesman called Prideaux. French-derived names are common in North Devon; there was an influx of Huguenots from France in 1685 when they were being persecuted.

THE PANNIER MARKET 1903 49622
This was built in 1855, along with Butchers Row. Again, the man responsible was R D Gould. Designed for traders to display their wares in panniers, the building is essentially unchanged today.

◆

BUTCHERS' ROW 1919 69323
There were originally 33 small shops in Butchers' Row. The architectural flair and panache associated with Victorian work is evidenced here. The pilasters are in Bath stone, with elegant wrought iron roof supports. The traders' names have now changed, but many are still open fronted and thriving, doubtless awaiting the dead hand of EC regulation to sanitise them. The auctioneers at the end, on Boutport Street, is now the tourist information office. The Pannier Market is to the left.

THE PANNIER MARKET 1903 49622

BUTCHERS' ROW 1919 69323

THE PANNIER MARKET 1919 69324
A busy day at the market, note the
people to the front of the crowd are
posing for the photographer.

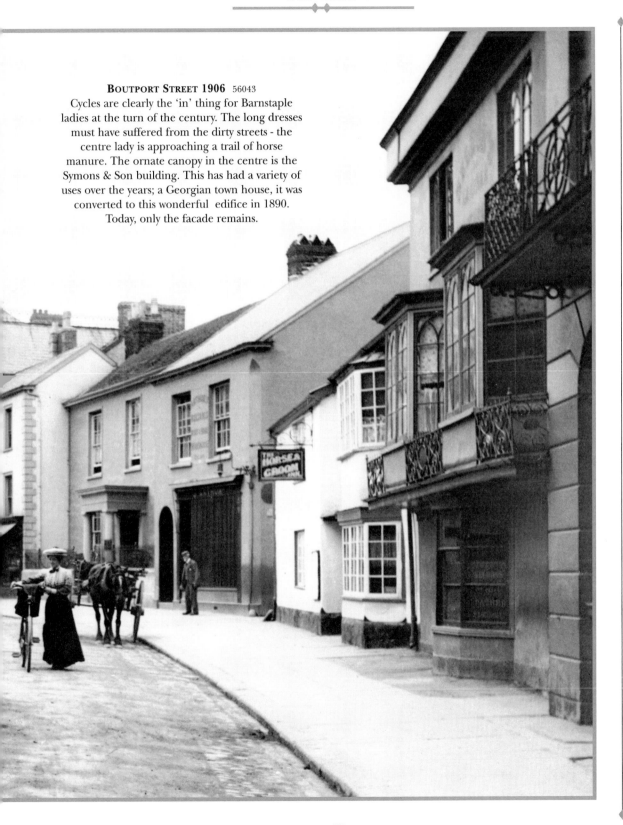

BOUTPORT STREET 1906 56043
Cycles are clearly the 'in' thing for Barnstaple ladies at the turn of the century. The long dresses must have suffered from the dirty streets - the centre lady is approaching a trail of horse manure. The ornate canopy in the centre is the Symons & Son building. This has had a variety of uses over the years; a Georgian town house, it was converted to this wonderful edifice in 1890. Today, only the facade remains.

BOUTPORT STREET 1919 69322

The Horse and Groom together with the next two buildings made way for a road; the Queens Head inn now occupies a corner of the new road - Queen Street. Clarkes printing works survived, as the following view shows. On the left, the tall chimney was attached to the Albert Hall - now The Queens Theatre.

BOUTPORT STREET C1965 B25102

Now, an architecturally unsympathetic post office occupies the corner of Queen Street/Boutport Street, Clarkes printing works has become Clarkes Hotel and Symons has lost its glorious canopy. A Ford Cortina and a Vauxhall, together with a Morris delivery van can be seen on the road.

BEAR STREET c1955

Looking away from Boutport Street, little has changed. The shop on the right - Beer and Greenslade - appears to be selling cycles. The name has changed, but the product has not. Fish and chips are also still available, even if the sign is now much lower.

BEAR STREET AND THE POST OFFICE c1955

All has changed. The inner relief road carved through here a decade ago from left to right, destroying the post office and the surrounding houses. The Stag's Head and (partially obscured by the tree) the monumental masons -Youing's - survive on the corner of the new road.

BEAR STREET c1955 B25009

BEAR STREET AND THE POST OFFICE c1955 B25008

BEAR STREET c1955 B25007
From further up Bear Street, we see what was demolished to allow the new road through. Beyond the bow windows is now mechanised mayhem. The delivery truck parked on the left hand side is outside the post office. The Ford Popular car seems to want all the road

EBBERLY LAWN c1955 B25012

Looking back over the Lawn towards Bear Street, the view is instantly recognisable today. The road is widened a little and the street furniture changed. It presents a delightful area of green close to the town centre and is a prized area to live.

THE GREEN c1871 5827

The Green is now built over. This picture shows the Union Workhouse. Subsequently, it would become the Alexandra Hospital, which remained in business until 1978 when the new North Devon General hospital was opened.

THE IMPERIAL HOTEL 1900 45717
A scene of studied elegance outside the Imperial
Hotel. Under the white tent (left) rustic chairs are
provided for guests. There are also plenty of seats
around the well-tended grounds which allow
ample opportunity for breaks whilst taking the air.

THE IMPERIAL HOTEL 1912 64572

A large extension to the hotel was needed to cope with the massive influx of tourists that increasing holiday allowances and the railways had created. The original building is to the left. Blinds are fitted to the upper windows. These are west-facing and are likely to be affected by a strong sunset in summer. The rustic thatched shed survived into recent memory.

THE ALMSHOUSES 1903 49625

There are twenty almshouses in the Lichdon Street group. They were founded by John Penrose, a cloth merchant of the town (and mayor in 1620), in 1627. The low porticoes have granite pillars and the stone-built design offers an insight into architectural practices of the era.

ROCK PARK 1890 24864

ROCK PARK 1890 24864
In 1863 the mayor, J R Chanter, had created a small park from reclaimed land. Then, in 1879, William Rock, a local man who went to London and made a fortune, returned home to improve Barnstaple. He bought up the surrounding area, old industrial and housing land, to create the Park. Given to the town, it is above the bridge on the town side. Note the collection of perambulators and baby carriages under the tree. One lady sports a nanny's outfit.

ROCK PARK 1935 86661
The thatched bandstand was not built when the Park was opened, but was added as part of Queen Victoria's Diamond Jubilee celebrations. It was regularly used, and featured particularly in the town's Millenary celebrations in 1930. In the early 1960s, it was deemed unsafe and demolished.

ROCK PARK 1935 86661

ROCK PARK C1955 B25069
Taw Vale Road has changed somewhat since this picture was taken. The Ford garage, Taw Vale Motors, occupies what was Hopgood Haulage Contractors. This view was taken from the raised South Walk. Then, as now, it is a popular place for mothers to take their children out in prams: you don't see so many nannies these days though.

St Peters Church 1929 82268

St Peter's is the parish church of Barnstaple. This present building was erected in the 13th century on the site of a previous church. The curious broach spire - one of three in North Devon - was added in 1389, paid for by the corporation. S. Peter's was restored in the 17th century and again in 1866, this time by Sir Gilbert Scott.

THE CROOKED SPIRE, THE PARISH CHURCH 1936 87550

Not only Chesterfield in Derbyshire has a crooked spire. Theirs may be more famous, but St Peter's has quite a pronounced twist. Its survival is due to Sir Gilbert Scott's putting his foot down most firmly. When a complete rebuild was proposed, he threatened to withdraw if the spire was removed. The drapers shop (left) has a selection of patterns for both dressmakers and knitters in the window. The wrought iron gate survived the last war.

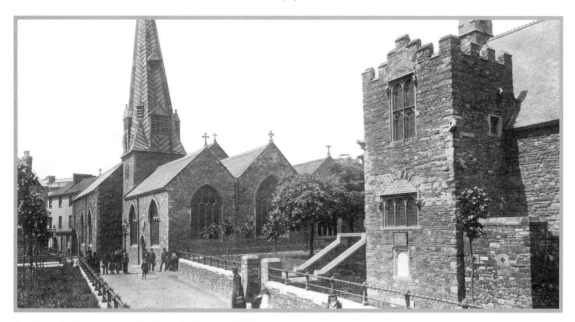

ST PETER'S CHURCH AND ST ANNE'S CHAPEL 1890 24873

The lower parts of the chapel were built in 1330 as a charnel house, but it became a chantry chapel, endowed by John Holman, in 1449. Edward VI dissolved all chantry chapels in 1549 and the building eventually came into corporation ownership. They created a grammar school. It was also used at weekends by Huguenot refugees as a church and survived as a school into the last century. It now houses a museum.

THE PARISH CHURCH 1919 69319

The pleasing interior of the church is the result of Sir Gilbert Scott's work. He had the choir stalls re-arranged to allow more space. The pulpit to the left is stone, a gift from a parishioner, and was installed at the time of the last restoration in 1866.

ST. MARY MAGDALENE'S CHURCH WALK 1919 69317
Strange though it may seem in this fin de siecle moral climate, St Mary Magdalene's was built because, in the early 19th century, the parish church could not handle the number of worshippers. Then, it was common practice for people to have their own pew reserved; newcomers simply could not get in. Therefore this church was built in 1846. The beautiful arcade of trees made a delightful approach to the building.

St. Mary Magdalene's Church 1919 69316

The church was located along Bear Street and had a quite brief lifespan. With numbers of worshippers falling dramatically, and the prospect of the inner relief road being built, it was knocked down in 1980: a sadly short life for such a wonderful building, as this interior view will confirm.

Bishops Tawton, The Village 1890 24886

Once a sleepy hamlet, Bishops Tawton is now a coveted area for Barnstaple commuters. The church, St John the Baptist is essentially 14th century, although much of the interior has been re-modelled. The river Taw runs through the plain behind the smoking chimney, with Tawstock beyond.

BRAUNTON
Old House, Church Street 1900 45685
As much as any other, this view illustrates the timelessness of North Devon. Hang a B & B sign in front of the left-hand house, add a telephone pole, turn the downstairs window in the main house into a door covered by a pretty porch and, a century later, there is the view. Sadly, the children's delightful pinafores are consigned to history. Every one of the well-dressed children wears a hat: only the rather scruffy boy to the left is bare headed.

BRAUNTON, NORTH STREET 1900 45686
Although some of the cob and thatch buildings have been replaced, there are still examples to be seen, and North Street is narrow to this day. When this picture was taken, the road was still unsurfaced and rainwater drainage non-existent. It must have been most unpleasantly muddy after rain or dusty in sunny weather.

CROYDE, THE BAY 1894 33432

Once a sleepy Devon backwater, Croyde's beach and bay was discovered by holidaymakers in the 19th century. With two huge caravan parks, this area fills up dramatically in the short summer season. Here we see an altogether quieter scene. Laver seaweed grows on the rocks: picked, boiled and served with bacon for breakfast it has a wonderful flavour - albeit something of an acquired taste.

CROYDE, THE BAY AND BAGGY POINT 1936 87581

This view is taken from Saunton Down over the popular holiday beach at Croyde. In the field below, the wheat is harvested and placed in stooks to dry. This was before combine harvesters were used. The area above and to the right of the farmhouse is now a massive holiday park.

CROYDE, OLD COTTAGES 1936 87584

The hedgerow seems to hold fascination for the two youngsters. Was it the blackberry season? The narrow street leading towards Georgeham has changed little in the intervening years, although the stream has a more formal channel today.

FREMINGTON, THE CHURCH c1955 F100001

Much of the quaintness of St Peter's was lost when Sir Gilbert Scott 'restored' it in 1867. But the Norman tower was unaffected. It is believed that there was once a spire atop this. Just inside the door is a Norman holy water stoup - a small stone basin.

FREMINGTON, THE MAIN ROAD c1955 F100002

This scene is hardly recognisable today. The wall on the right was knocked down and a garage built. This disappeared in 1997, replaced by a pretty park. The Post Office has gone, and the Westward Ho! based Buckleigh Laundry is now called Buckleigh Linen Service. The furthest building, The New Inn, still serves splendid meals. The two motor bikes look as though they belong to campers; perhaps they are calling for liquid refreshment in those pre-breathalyser days.

FREMINGTON, THE VILLAGE c1955 F100006

Off the main road, Fremington has changed little. The man standing in the doorway would undoubtedly recognise the scene today, even if the shop has closed and is now Penny Cottage. Thatch is still a major roofing material in Fremington, and it is often possible to see the thatcher at his work. At the end, the building at right angles is The New Inn.

GOODLEIGH, THE CHURCH 1894 33426

LANDKEY, THE VILLAGE c1955 L193016

GOODLEIGH, THE CHURCH 1894
Plain and unostentatious: this seems only
way to describe St Gregory's church. It
had been extensively rebuilt a mere
decade before this picture was taken.
One unusual feature is that the windows
have clear glass.

◆

LANDKEY, THE VILLAGE c1955
Before the link road between the M5
and Barnstaple was built, Landkey was
on the main road out of North Devon.
Its long, straggly nature is clear from this
photograph. Note the old 'school' traffic
sign on the recessed wall to the left. The
symbol then was a flaming torch, its
detail picked out with white reflectors.

LANDKEY, THE CHURCH c1885 L193301

This delightful building is late 15th-century with very little alteration. The thatched linhay was ubiquitous at the time of this picture. Today, they are hard to find. Are the cows thin versions of the shorthorn, the standard milk cow of the era? The area in front of the church is now filled with tombstones.

SAUNTON, THE SANDS 1920 69406

This area of the North Devon coast has acres of sandhills. These, at Saunton, were riddled with tiny beach chalets. Many survived until relatively recent times. The 'proper' housing lines the Braunton to Croyde road, and the sea (behind the camera) is a noted surfing area.

SAUNTON, THE SANDS 1938 88750
Even today, shrimping is still a popular pastime on the waterfront. The girl's bathing costume has legs to it; today's toddler is quite likely to be sporting a pair of knickers at most. The white building right of centre is the Saunton Sands Hotel. Today, this is expanded into a prestigious establishment, still white and gloriously floodlit at night.

SHIRWELL, THE VILLAGE c1955 S357024
There was once a Shirwell Hundred - that ancient administrative division of English counties that was supposed to contain a hundred families or freemen. On the outlying slopes of Exmoor, the village today is charming and, superficially at least, little changed from this photograph.

SHIRWELL
The Church c1955

Originally 15th century, St Paul's has been greatly restored, but it still offers a couple of treasures inside. One is the tomb of Lady Ann Chichester who died in 1723. A branch of the famed family lived nearby for over 400 years from 1490; round-the-world yachtsman Sir Francis Chichester was one member.

◆

SWIMBRIDGE
The Village c1890

Swimbridge was the next village along the Barnstaple to South Molton road after Landkey. In the picture, there are roadside poles. Are they for gas lighting, or telephones even? Certainly not electricity. In the bottom left corner is the Jack Russell inn.

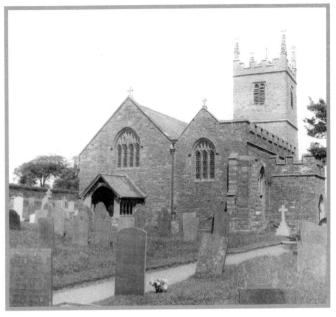

SHIRWELL, THE CHURCH c1955 S357029

SWIMBRIDGE, THE VILLAGE c1890 S241301

SWIMBRIDGE, THE VILLAGE 1900 45724

A decade after the previous photograph, it is hard to find any alterations. A similar picture today would reveal far more changes. Looking north, the road runs close to the church whilst a back lane to Yarnacott - in the distance - climbs out of the valley. The thatched building on the left with a tall chimney has a black area on the roof; is it fire damage? A Sheet? Certainly, it does not appear on the previous picture.

SWIMBRIDGE, THE VILLAGE c1955 S241004

The two previous pictures looked north towards a hill, from which this view is taken. Of note is the amount of tree surgery that has taken place, particularly around the church. The main road towards South Molton is plain to see.

SWIMBRIDGE, THE CHURCH 1894 33428

Here is another broach spire, 102ft tall, after the style of St Peter's, Barnstaple. The church, St James, is packed with interest. The stone pulpit is 15th century, as is the beautiful rood screen, restored about 1880. Between 1832 and 1880, the curate here was John (Jack) Russell. He was the hunting parson who developed a new breed of terrier which was named after him.

SWIMBRIDGE, THE TANNERY c1955 S241009

The Tannery is no more, but the buildings have been converted to residential use. Above the white roofed building, The Jubilee Parish Hall, is an area of land that was actually a tennis court. The building to the left is the village shop, which we see in the next picture.

SWIMBRIDGE, THE POST OFFICE AND VILLAGE c1955 S241002

Looking towards Barnstaple, the village shop is still in business, albeit not selling Dominion Petrol any longer. Neither are the milk churns collected each day. Note also the metal hoarding advertising Westward Ho Smoking Mixture. The house to the right has been rebuilt, with the building line preserved.

TAWSTOCK, TAWSTOCK COURT 1890 24881
This house was built in 1787 by Sir Bourchier Wrey to replace a 16th-century building that was destroyed by fire. Its 'Gothick' design is conspicuous in a particularly beautiful corner of Devon, alongside the river Taw. Today, it has become St Michael's Independent and Day Boarding School, a much-respected educational establishment.

TAWSTOCK, THE CHURCH 1890 24882
This remarkable church, St Peter's, is hidden in the Taw valley a couple of miles from Barnstaple. Cruciform in plan, it is early 14th-century (one of only seven remaining in Devon) and contains the finest collection of monuments in the county.

Index

The Surrounding Area

Frith Book Co 1999 Titles

From 2000 we aim at publishing 100 new books each year. For latest catalogue please contact Frith Book Co

Barnstaple	1-85937-084-5	£12.99	Oct 99
Blackpool	1-85937-049-7	£12.99	Sep 99
Bognor Regis	1-85937-055-1	£12.99	Sep 99
Bristol	1-85937-050-0	£12.99	Sep 99
Cambridge	1-85937-092-6	£12.99	Oct 99
Cambridgeshire	1-85937-086-1	£14.99	Nov 99
Cheshire	1-85937-045-4	£14.99	Sep 99
Chester	1-85937-090-X	£12.99	Nov 99
Chesterfield	1-85937-071-3	£12.99	Sep 99
Chichester	1-85937-089-6	£12.99	Nov 99
Cornwall	1-85937-054-3	£14.99	Sep 99
Cotswolds	1-85937-099-3	£14.99	Nov 99

Maidstone	1-85937-056-X	£12.99	Sep 99
Northumberland & Tyne and Wear	1-85937-072-1	£14.99	Sep 99
North Yorkshire	1-85937-048-9	£14.99	Sep 99
Nottingham	1-85937-060-8	£12.99	Sep 99
Oxfordshire	1-85937-076-4	£14.99	Oct 99
Penzance	1-85937-069-1	£12.99	Sep 99
Reading	1-85937-087-X	£12.99	Nov 99
St Ives	1-85937-068-3	£12.99	Sep 99
Salisbury	1-85937-091-8	£12.99	Nov 99
Scarborough	1-85937-104-3	£12.99	Sep 99
Scottish Castles	1-85937-077-2	£14.99	Oct 99
Sevenoaks and Tonbridge	1-85937-057-8	£12.99	Sep 99
Sheffield and S Yorkshire	1-85937-070-5	£12.99	Sep 99
Shropshire	1-85937-083-7	£14.99	Nov 99
Southampton	1-85937-088-8	£12.99	Nov 99
Staffordshire	1-85937-047-0	£14.99	Sep 99
Stratford upon Avon	1-85937-098-5	£12.99	Nov 99
Suffolk	1-85937-074-8	£14.99	Oct 99
Surrey	1-85937-081-0	£14.99	Oct 99
Torbay	1-85937-063-2	£12.99	Sep 99
Wiltshire	1-85937-053-5	£14.99	Sep 99

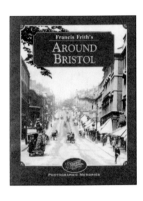

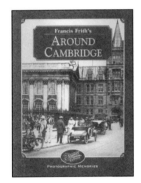

Derby	1-85937-046-2	£12.99	Sep 99
Devon	1-85937-052-7	£14.99	Sep 99
Dorset	1-85937-075-6	£14.99	Oct 99
Dorset Coast	1-85937-062-4	£14.99	Sep 99
Dublin	1-85937-058-6	£12.99	Sep 99
East Anglia	1-85937-059-4	£14.99	Sep 99
Eastbourne	1-85937-061-6	£12.99	Sep 99
English Castles	1-85937-078-0	£14.99	Oct 99
Essex	1-85937-082-9	£14.99	Nov 99
Falmouth	1-85937-066-7	£12.99	Sep 99
Hampshire	1-85937-064-0	£14.99	Sep 99
Hertfordshire	1-85937-079-9	£14.99	Nov 99
Isle of Man	1-85937-065-9	£14.99	Sep 99
Liverpool	1-85937-051-9	£12.99	Sep 99

British Life A Century Ago

246 x 189mm 144pp, hardback. Black and white Lavishly illustrated with photos from the turn of the century, and with extensive commentary. It offers a unique insight into the social history and heritage of bygone Britain.

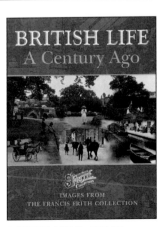

1-85937-103-5 £17.99 ....

Available from your local bookshop or from the publisher

FRITH PRODUCTS & SERVICES

Francis Frith would doubtless be pleased to know that the pioneering publishing venture he started in 1860 still continues today. More than a hundred and thirty years later, The Francis Frith Collection continues in the same innovative tradition and is now one of the foremost publishers of vintage photographs in the world. Some of the current activities include:

Interior Decoration

Today Frith's photographs can be seen framed and as giant wall murals in thousands of pubs, restaurants, hotels, banks, retail stores and other public buildings throughout the country. In every case they enhance the unique local atmosphere of the places they depict and provide reminders of gentler days in an increasingly busy and frenetic world.

Product Promotions

Frith products have been used by many major companies to promote the sales of their own products or to reinforce their own history and heritage. Brands include Hovis bread, Courage beers, Scots Porage Oats, Colman's mustard, Cadbury's foods, Mellow Birds coffee, Dunhill pipe tobacco, Guinness, and Bulmer's Cider.

Genealogy and Family History

As the interest in family history and roots grows world-wide, more and more people are turning to Frith's photographs of Great Britain for images of the towns, villages and streets where their ancestors lived; and, of course, photographs of the churches and chapels where their ancestors were christened, married and buried are an essential part of every genealogy tree and family album.

A series of easy-to-use CD Roms is planned for publication, and an increasing number of Frith photographs will be able to be viewed on specialist genealogy sites. A growing range of Frith books will be available on CD.

The Internet

Already thousands of Frith photographs can be viewed and purchased on the internet. By the end of the year 2000 some 60,000 Frith photographs will be available on the internet. The number of sites is constantly expanding, each focussing on different products and services from the Collection.

Some of the sites are listed below.

www.townpages.co.uk
www.familystorehouse.com
www.britannia.com
www.icollector.com
www.barclaysquare.co.uk
www.cornwall-online.co.uk

For background information on the Collection look at the two following sites:

www.francisfrith.com
www.francisfrith.co.uk

Frith Products

All Frith photographs are available Framed or just as Mounted Prints, and can be ordered from the address below. From time to time other products - Address Books, Calendars, Table Mats, Postcards etc - are available.

The Frith Collectors' Guild

In response to the many customers who enjoy collecting Frith photographs we have created the Frith Collectors' Guild. Members are entitled to a range of benefits, including a regular magazine, special discounts and special limited edition products.

For further information: if you would like further information on any of the above aspects of the Frith business please contact us at the address below:

The Francis Frith Collection, Frith's Barn, Teffont, Salisbury, Wiltshire England SP3 5QP.
Tel: +44 (0) 1722 716 376 Fax: +44 (0) 1722 716 881 Email: frithbook.co.uk

To receive your FREE Mounted Print

Cut out this Voucher and return it with your remittance for £1.50 to cover postage and handling. Choose any photograph included in this book. Your SEPIA print will be A4 in size, and mounted in a cream mount with burgundy rule lines, overall size 14 x 11 inches.

Order additional Mounted Prints at HALF PRICE (only £7.49 each*)

If there are further pictures you would like to order, possibly as gifts for friends and family, acquire them at half price (no additional postage and handling required).

Have your Mounted Prints framed*

For an additional £14.95 per print you can have your chosen Mounted Print framed in an elegant polished wood and gilt moulding, overall size 16 x 13 inches (no additional postage and handling required).

---

* IMPORTANT!
These special prices are only available if ordered using the original voucher on this page (no copies permitted) and at the same time as your free Mounted Print, for delivery to the same address

---

Frith Collectors' Guild

From time to time we publish a magazine of news and stories about Frith photographs and further special offers of Frith products. If you would like 12 months FREE membership, please return this form and we will send you a New Member Pack.

Send completed forms to:
The Francis Frith Collection,
Frith's Barn, Teffont, Salisbury,
Wiltshire SP3 5QP

Voucher for FREE and Reduced Price Frith Prints

Picture no.	Page number	Qty	Mounted @ £7.49	Framed + £14.95	Total Cost
		1	**Free of charge***	£	£
			£	£	£
			£	£	£
			£	£	£
			£	£	£
			£	£	£

Title: AROUND BARNSTAPLE
084-5

* Post & handling	£1.50
Total Order Cost	£

Please do not photocopy this voucher. Only the original is valid, so please cut it out and return it to us.

I enclose a cheque / postal order for £ . . . .
made payable to 'The Francis Frith Collection'
OR please debit my Mastercard / Visa / Switch / Amex card

Number . . . .

Expires . . . . Signature . . . .

Name Mr/Mrs/Ms . . . .

Address . . . .

. . . .

. . . .

. . . . Postcode . . . .

Daytime Tel No . . . .   Valid to 31/12/01

The Francis Frith Collectors' Guild

I would like to receive the New Members Pack offering 12 months FREE membership.

084-5

Name Mr/Mrs/Ms . . . .

Address . . . .

. . . .

. . . . Postcode . . . .

Free Print - see overleaf